The Ultimate Monologue Book
for Middle School Actors Volume III

111 One-Minute Monologues

A Smith and Kraus Book
Published by Smith and Kraus, Inc.
177 Lyme Road, Hanover, NH 03755
www.smithkraus.com

First Edition: January 2005
Manufactured in the United States of America
10 9 8 7 6 5 4 3 2 1

Cover and text design by Julia Gignoux, Freedom Hill Design

Library of Congress Cataloging-in-Publication Data
L. E. McCullough.
111 one-minute monologues / L. E. McCullough —1st ed.
p. cm. — (The ultimate audition book for middle school actors ; 3)
(Young actors series)
Summary: A collection of 111 original monologues, each about one minute long, to
be used by male and female middle school actors for auditions and other purposes.
ISBN 1-57525-419-0 (vol. 3)
1. Monologues—Juvenile literature. 2. Acting—Juvenile literature. [1. Monologues.
2. Acting.] I. Title: One hundred and eleven one-minute monologues. II. Title. III.
Series. IV. Young actor series.

PN2080.D33 2003
812'.6—dc22
2003057251

The Ultimate Monologue Book for Middle School Actors VOLUME III

• • •

111 One-Minute Monologues

L. E. McCullough

YOUNG ACTORS SERIES

A Smith and Kraus Book

ACKNOWLEDGMENTS

Marilyn Moore, Guidepost Books; Susan Drury, Dramatists Guild Fund; Charles Michael, The Voice Bank; Diane Weisenberg, C.P.A.; Carol Cukras; Julie Ellen Prusinowski, New Jersey State Council on the Arts; Bob Higbie; the new generation of preteens past and present among the Abbate, Bansavage, Billet, Greeby, Horvay, Manion, McCullough, Robinson, Valenziano, and Willis families.

DEDICATION

To my parents, who helped me survive and flourish during my own wonderful, woeful, excruciating, exhilarating preteen years.

To my wife, Lisa Bansavage, who like myself is still and in many ways will forever be twelve years old at heart; her emotional acuity helped channel this book from the dim recesses of misty memory.

CONTENTS

Female Monologues

Male Monologues

Female/Male Monologues

DRAMA

Introduction

What you've got here are 111 different characters speaking in the distinct voices of early twenty-first-century human beings aged ten to fourteen — aka *preteens*.

Or does the term *preteen* cover ages ten to thirteen? Or nine to twelve? Or nine to thirteen? Or ten to fifteen, the age range the National Middle School Association considers the extended domain of preteendom, with the middle school experience serving as the defining transition period for children growing into young adulthood.

Don't worry about where you fit in this ever-evolving demographic. *You* know when you're a preteen because things (parents, friends, the world, you, *especially* you) just suddenly seem different than they were when you were a little kid. Being a preteen is all about discovery, and the characters in this book express the wonder, puzzlement, misery, elation, all the emotional extremes and intellectual flights of fancy that arise naturally when childhood collides with emerging teenhood.

These monologues cover a wide range of situations, emotions, and people. Read them through, find what feels good to you, what feels right for your experience or the character you want to inhabit and express. Feel free to incorporate movement when it enhances your character realization. Some setup directions have been provided to enhance your understanding of the situation and event sequence, and you'll likely mime these, unless you really do have a basketball or cell phone or soft drink bottle handy. But to develop better acting technique, you should strive to do the monologue without props. It's a skill that will come in handy when you're at an audition and handed a fresh side that says: "Walking on a tight rope above Grand Canyon carrying a stuffed platinum mongoose."

Nearly three-quarters of these monologues are suitable for either male or female actors, and even some marked specifically "male" or "female" can be easily altered. Feel free to change a word or two here and there, if needed, and to adapt a monologue to your gender, hometown, or personal history or situation or favorite pop star or video game. The more *personal* the monologue is to you, the more *power* you can summon in your delivery.

Why? Because power and personality are two things that define a monologue. A good monologue, a monologue that captures and holds the attention of your listeners, is all about *character*, all about crystallizing for just a few vital moments the essence of a character and expressing that essence in a novel, exciting, memorable manner.

A good monologue is an *effective* monologue, effective in compelling your audience to listen to you and only you, to be caught up and confined totally in the Moment of You. And yet at the same time to be transported beyond you to other people, other places, other times. Maybe even transported somewhere deep inside themselves . . . a place they might seldom venture, or thought they'd forgotten, or wondered if they'd ever reach.

The key to unlocking the character in a monologue? *Language*. Each one of us on this planet uses language in a distinctive way that expresses our uniqueness as thinking, sentient beings. The language we choose to relate to the world — and to ourselves — reveals much about who we think we are and who we think we can be. When combined with appropriate gesture and intonation, words allow the character in a monologue to emerge and take shape before your very eyes.

Above all, have fun meeting 111 new people. Each one of these monologues *is* a person, and each is waiting to talk to you, eager to let you know what's on his orher mind. Listen, and you'll definitely learn a few things about each world — and yours.

L. E. McCullough, Ph.D.
Director, Children's Playwriting Institute
Woodbridge, New Jersey

Female Monologues

. . .

COMEDY

HEARD IT THROUGH THE WEBVINE

(Typing on keyboard.) Yes, ma'am. No, ma'am. *(Looks up defiantly.)* But Shana blogged me first! She set up a Web site that had a picture of my head stuck on a rhinoceros body. And the body was wearing *my* Lilo and Stitch bathing suit! *(Typing on keyboard.)* Yes, ma'am. No, ma'am. *(Head lowered contritely.)* It was wrong of me to use the school computer to send Shana's e-mail address to the International Avon Dealers list. *(Giggles.)* She's still getting spam from eighty-nine countries and fifteen time zones! Haw! *(Stifles, resumes typing.)* Yes, ma'am. No, ma'am. I don't call that behavior something a best friend would do to another best friend. But we're not best friends anymore. Haven't you heard? She sent a text message to the whole school saying she's best friends with Emily! Emily, whose daddy just bought her her own broadband network!

SLEEPOVER

(Waves cheerily.) Hi, Kimberly! So glad you could sleep over! *(Aside.)* Mom said if I didn't invite her, I couldn't have the party. I was like, Mo-ommmm! I haven't hung with Kimberly since fourth grade! We are worlds apart! I'm *NSYNC, she's Backstreet Boys. I'm Coke, she's Pepsi. I'm *CosmoGirl*, she's *Teen-Vogue*. I'm dELIA and she is *sooooo* K-Mart. I mean, Kimberly has a right to exist, I guess, and pursue as normal a life as someone with her brand-name tastes can. But, puhleeeeze . . . not at *my* sleepover!

FIRST KISS

There's this whole mystery about your first kiss. You know, what it's going to feel like when it happens with a boy you've thought about kissing for a while. I think it's going to taste like strawberry sherbet. OK, with maybe a thin layer of white chocolate in the middle to keep it rich and tender, light but filling with a tangy aftertaste depending on what mouthwash he's using. And it's going to smell like the perfume Mom wears on special occasions to go out with Dad, sweet but fresh like an expensive brand of rug deodorizer. And inside — inside I'm going to feel like I'm floating on a white fluffy cloud in a perfect blue sky. *(Closes eyes.)* Or maybe being carried away on a raft down a rushing waterfall. There will be music — a sweet, dreamy ballad by O-Town — and my whole body will be sizzling and chilling at the same time like I'm in a tanning bed filled with ice cubes, and suddenly, my heart will boil over and race pounding through my bloodstream till I nearly explode! And then I'll sigh. *(Sighs.)* Deeply. *(Sighs more deeply.)* Wow! *(Opens eyes.)* Wonder what the second kiss is like?

DREAM JOB

When I was a little kid, my parents helped me put up a lemonade stand on our street. I don't remember selling much lemonade that day. Might have been because we ran out of lemon juice and used melted white cheese spread. But that gave me a taste for running my own business someday. And now that I'm on the verge of almost entering the minimum-wage teen work force, I've been thinking about my dream job: I'd like to sell stuff at a kiosk in the mall. Mostly, I'd like to work at the crystal kiosk. I'd be surrounded by hundreds of crystals that hang and twirl and glimmer and shine! Everywhere I looked, there would be tinkling, gleaming pretty things! And I would learn the natural energy power of crystals. My crystals would set mental snares to pull shoppers into my psychic orbit. I'd meet fascinating people. And they'd give me money. *Lots* of money. People, power, money — where do I apply?

MY LIFE IS OVER

I have a bit of advice for anyone looking to survive middle school with a minimum of psychological scarring. Never play Truth or Dare. And if you do, never, *never* tell the Truth! Last night when my turn came up, I was going to choose Dare. But the turn before, Marla Whittaker dared Sunni Ramos to hop around like a frog shouting, "I love shopping at Goodwill!" That is so immature, and I vowed never to let Marla borrow my Powerpuff Girls Denim Lunchbox Handbag ever again. So I chose Truth and had to tell who I had a supersecret crush on. I still don't know why I didn't say the name of a fictional person, like Newt Gingrich or Madonna. But I got caught up in the whole truth and honesty thing and said, "I have a crush on Dennis Pearson in home room! Truth!" Next day, it was all over the entire school. And Dennis just looked at me like I was some kind of bug had landed on his lunch. My life is over. And that's no lie.

STYLE POINTS

(Looks in mirror, smooths hair, tweaks clothing.) About a month ago, I started working on my style points. You know, dressing a little better, a little more popular. Caring about, you know, little things. Like, to make your lips seem fuller, put a teense of shimmer right in the center of your lower lip. Just a little thing, right? But pretty soon, I see guys notice me, looking at me different than before. And they notice I see them noticing. Except now I see my girlfriends notice guys noticing me. And they won't talk to me at all!

THE ONLY RATIONAL EXPLANATION

Something happened to me this first year of middle school. Something unexpected, tragic, and — to a sensitive preteen like myself — emotionally devastating. I think I stopped being fun. My friend Mandee had a slumber party at her house last weekend. Did I bring along a stack of fashion magazines to look through so we could give each other makeovers? Noooooo. Did I pack an awesome party-mix CD? Noooooo. I brought a travel alarm clock, so I wouldn't sleep too late the next day. What was I thinking? Next day when Maria and I were cruising the mall and met a couple of cute guys from another school, did I: (a) "accidentally" bump into the cutest one and start a conversation? (b) ask him to help me pick out something for my brother's birthday, even though I don't actually have nor want a brother? Or (c) remind Maria we have a ten o'clock curfew and have to get back home right away? You guessed it. Choice C for "clueless"! I think I've started to turn into a grown-up. Alien abduction is the only rational explanation. Somebody stop me before I adultify again!

THAT'S GRATITUDE FOR YOU

Call me radical. Call me righteous. Call me really sick of listening to my friend yak about her gorgeous movie-star hair all the time. You wouldn't believe the attention she gets from kids at school! Even grown-ups: "Oh, Larissa, your hair is so lush, so lustrous, so lovable!" It drives me loony! So, when I was at her house last week — you're thinking I waited till she was asleep and then cut off her hair, right? *Wrong!* And shame on you! What kind of weirdos are you people? I simply went into the bathroom and put a few drops of green food coloring in her shampoo. *(Giggles.)* Next day at school, that lush, lustrous, lovable Larissa hair was as green as a pickle dipped in green paint on St. Patrick's Day! Hah! You can't believe the attention her hair got now! You can't believe the stares, the pointing, the looks of pure, unadulterated . . . admiration! Within a week every girl in class tinted their hair green to copy Larissa. She became the style queen of the entire school! And not one word of thanks to me!

PUT TOGETHER

(Standing in front of mirror, inspecting hair and face.) Big dance tonight. I've got to get put together. Let's see. I'll do my hair like Shiri, or no — like Alyssa, she looked so swerve in *Charmed*. Jessica Simpson uses this shampoo, I saw that in *Sugar*. This curling iron was endorsed by Katie Holmes, did you see that on *E!*? She's my fave! OK, I want my brows like Julia in *My Best Friend's Wedding* and nose like Nicole in *Moulin Rouge*. Mmm-hmm, a little eyeliner from LeeLee, a dab of J-Lo's foundation, OK, and some blush by Britney. Bronzer courtesy of Ms. Angelina ought to top that off. Now, the lips, hmmm. . . definitely not the night for Courtney, maybe Cameron, no, wait — need a serious pout, call in the big doggette, Shannen! Annnnnd with lip gloss from Reese, girl, you are so perfectly put together! That's what I like best about getting older: You finally can discover who you really are.

THE MOST LOGICAL THING

My friend and I are crushing on the same guy. I think he likes me better, though. Should I tell my friend? Let's look at this logically; there's a deep, deep friendship on the line here. I'll try walking a mile in her shoes. *(Swerves awkwardly in place.)* OK, I'm Julia. I'm thinking like Julia, and I think this guy is a total hottie. My new summer outfits will look so good with him on my arm. And I deserve him because I am pure butter — not like skanky Gina, who *thinks* she's my best friend. Hah! It is to mirth! I, Julia, am the bling-bling; I, Julia, am the hoochie queen; I, Julia, am the player shorty! I want, I need, I desire, me-me-me-me-me! *(Stops marching.)* You know, this is a lot of trouble for a starter crush. Maybe we should just do the most logical thing — flip a coin for him!

Female Monologues

· · ·

DRAMA

THINK WHAT OVER?

You just wanted to give me time to think things over. Uh-huh. Think what over? One day you're my boyfriend, next day you're not! Yes, I noticed! Hey, don't swear at me! Right, 'cause I'm so proper! You're not worthy to date a girl from Williams Creek! Is that what you think? Or are you just scared to tell me how you really feel? You use my family as an excuse. I'm not my parents, Steve. I'm me! Can't you tell the difference? Or do you want to?

I WANTED TO PLAY

(Dribbling basketball, setting for a shot.) I'm a good point guard, best on our team. Everybody says so, ask any girl in the league. But today, all-city championship on the line, I'll be riding the bench. *(Tosses ball up, catches it.)* Tara Bennett's going to take my place, even though she's three inches shorter, can't drive inside, and has a free throw percentage in single digits. Didn't make any sense to me, either, till Caitlin told me that Tara's mom donated a minivan to the school. And Tara's uncle is on the basketball camp scholarship committee. Whatever! *(Dribbles ball.)* I mostly wanted to play 'cause my dad is leaving for overseas duty tomorrow. *(Sets for shot.)* I wanted the last thing he saw me do be something I was really good at. *(Shoots.)*

CHAT ROOMMATES (TISHA)

My friend Melanie is always in the chat rooms. I know her user names in the chat rooms, and sometimes I'm in the same ones. I see her writing some really sick stuff about drugs and sex. When I ask her about it in school, she just laughs and says she's just making it up for fun. She says there's nothing wrong with making stuff up in a chat room with people you don't know and never see. But I worry about her. If I tell my parents and they tell her parents, she'll stop being my friend. If I don't tell, and she isn't just making it up, she could get into really bad trouble. I just don't know who the real Melanie is anymore. Whether it's my friend I sing with in church choir, or the stranger I hear cursing at people in the chat rooms.

CHAT ROOMMATES (MELANIE)

I try to get my friend Tisha to chill out. You're *supposed* to let yourself go a little crazy in a chat room. You can be somebody you're totally not, somebody you're afraid to be, maybe. Or ashamed to be. I pretend I'm old, around twenty. And blonde. And sometimes, divorced, or a dancer in a club with a hot red convertible. I have really wacko conversations with guys. They tell me a lot of secrets. Things kids at school sure don't talk about! Things I like to hear. Maybe someday I'll meet one of these guys, like at a mall on a dare. That is, if they *are* guys. In a chat room, they could be anybody, maybe even a girl like me. Who knows? Who cares? *(Laughs.)*

INSTANT MOM

Things are gonna get bad pretty soon. Mom got laid off again. That means she gets depressed and starts drinking. Or taking pills from the doctor that make her sleep a lot. Then I end up having to take care of my little brother and sister. I feed them, give them baths, everything Mom should be doing. I don't have time to do things after school or hang with friends or even walk to the park down the street. I become the "instant Mom." Oh, I know it's not fair. But what's fair got to do with it? I can't make it fair just by wishing for it, if I could I would, so quit bugging me about your fair crap, dammit!, 'cause it's not fair! *(Pauses, calms.)* Sorry. I was just practicing to be Mom again.

A DIFFERENT DREAM

My name is Essie — short for Esperanza, which in Spanish means *hope*. That was my name when we lived in Mexico, where I was born twelve years ago. Here in the United States, where I live now, people call me Essie. It is easier for my teachers to say than Esperanza. And better for our family, says my mother, until we get our residence papers in order.

For the last two months our family has lived in a motel on a busy highway outside a large city in the Midwest. Soon we will be moving to a state in the Northeast or maybe to Florida. Wherever we go, we will live in a motel like this one. If you were driving by on the highway, you would probably not notice this motel. Or care to stay there. The lights on the front sign are broken, and the outside walls need new paint. There is no swimming pool, and there is no room service. The rooms are small and most of the windows have cracks. To most Americans driving by, this motel looks like a tired old person in dusty gray clothes taking a nap.

But this motel has a secret. It has an entire Mexican village tucked away inside. In the room next to us is a *panadero*, a baker, who makes delicious tortillas. A *costurera* lives in that room and can sew anything you want from any piece of cloth you give her. Luis on the corner is a fine performer of the guitarron who plays music for our parties. Señora Valdez is a midwife who helps the women in the motel who cannot see a doctor when they are going to have a baby. The man who was the police chief of our village in Mexico lives across the courtyard. He fixes computers part-time, and his two sons work for a landscaper, also part-time.

More than one hundred Mexicanos live in this motel. They are busboys and cooks, maids and janitors. They pave driveways and dig ditches. They cut lawns and scrub dirt from the fountain at city hall. They take care of other people's babies and pets and grandparents. They are the people you see every day but never notice for more than a few moments. After work they disappear into the shadows, into motels like this all across America. There, for a few hours they can rest and dream they are back in Mexico.

But me, I have a different dream. I dream about going someday away to college. And coming back and becoming the mayor. A mayor who would make sure all the people in the town, no matter where they come from, got to live in a good house and have a good job. A mayor who would make sure all children felt welcome in their new school. A mayor who would never let anyone in the town live even one day without *esperanza* . . . hope.

IT'S ALL ABOUT LOVE

It's all about love. Really, I did it for love, ask anyone in the whole school. My boyfriend's birthday was coming up, and I didn't have any money for a present. But I really love him and wanted to get something that was totally awesome! So I took some old jewelry my gramma had left my mom, just a couple old rings and some scrubby bracelet, and pawned them at Ritter's. It's not like she ever wears them, and I figured I'd get them out of hock the next week, but they got sold. So that's my fault? Look, if I had a bigger allowance, it wouldn't have happened. And if I didn't love this guy so much! Look, maybe we could just say I learned a lot from the whole experience and leave it at that? I mean, if you love somebody, it's all right, right?

I WANT IMMATURE

The more time we spent with each other, the more he wanted to be with me. He started asking me not to go out with my friends so much. He said they encouraged me to party and flirt and be immature, which was true, kind of, I mean, we're only in middle school. I guess I was flattered 'cause I thought his being jealous meant he really loved me, so I stopped hanging with my friends. Only Stacy called me on it and said it was out of line. My other friends envied me, at first. They thought it was cool my boyfriend was so intense. I'm not so sure "intense" is something I want in my life right now. I want friends. I want immature.

GUESTS FOR THE HOLIDAYS

(Hands clasped behind back.) "Mama, can I ask you a question? I know I oughta be in bed, but, we've got guests." Mama looked past me into the living room and gasped. A man and a woman stood next to our Christmas tree. The man was tall and broad-shouldered, the woman short and thick around the waist. Their faces were swarthy, their clothes ragged and gypsylike. Illumination from the corner street lamp filtered in through the window behind them, framing their shapes with a soft contour of pale, glistening light.

Zoomer began to bark. "Hush that dog!" snapped Mama. She folded her arms over her chest and walked slowly back and forth in front of the couple, then stared at me. "Brenda Jean, just what gave you the idea to bring complete strangers into our house on Christmas Eve? Where's the phone, I'm callin' 911."

I moved in front of the phone table. "Their names is, um, well, I don't know their names 'cause they don't speak much English. But they're real nice and they got no place to go and it's so cold and can't they spend the night, Mama, please?"

The man took a half step forward. "I good worker. And my wife, she to have some baby. Soon." He put his arm around the woman, who smiled wanly at Mama and bowed her dark-eyed, scarf-shrouded head.

"They talk like they's from Russia or some dang place fulla foreigners," droned Mimaw, holding a mewing cat under each arm. "Bet they was sent here as spies and then lit out on their own. Look at 'em there, grinnin' like rattlesnakes in a nesta baby bluebirds!"

"Mimaw, that's mean!" I said.

"Brenda Jean, don't talk like that to your elders," Mama scolded. "Hand me that phone."

"Oh, Mama, puhleeeze!" I whimpered. "It's Christmas Eve!"

Mama had her hand out for the phone, then brought it up to her face and rubbed her tired eyes. "Guests for the holidays. Just what we need." She sighed, then snapped out a new set of orders. "Brenda Jean, go get that extra blanket in the closet. Mimaw, you go to your room. And take those dang cats with you."

GROUP DYNAMICS

Groups of friends can be tricky. Friendships within a group are almost never equal. Sometimes leaders just naturally emerge. Tell the truth now. You couldn't say, truthfully, that I'm the loudest of the group, could you? Or the boldest. Or even the smartest or hottest. But I am the one you turn to when you need advice. When you need guidance. When you need a true friend to help you with something that's hard for you to do, I'm there for you, aren't I? If you think we're running your life, well, you don't have to go along with everything the group says or does. In a real friendship there is always room for disagreement. But there isn't any disagreement here. You see it very clearly, don't you? Janet needs to be taught a lesson. A very harsh but permanent lesson that will help her fit in better with the group. And you're the best girl I know at delivering that kind of a lesson. *Presents object.)* Here, this is the knife. And this is to wipe up with and take to the incinerator. Tell the truth now. Aren't you glad you don't have to make decisions like this on your own?

COMFORTABLE GENES

Mom, I like doing things with you. I know other girls sometimes don't like hanging out with their moms, but I do, really.
And I appreciate you being concerned about my weight. OK,
about being "healthy," whatever, and, yes, I know the routine
about learning to be comfortable with your genes — G-E-N-
E-S. So you don't have to trick me into exercising. You don't
have to say, "Let's go the gym together and get ready for bikini
season!" I'm not going to be ready for bikini season. Not this
season, probably not any season ever. I'm OK with that. I'm
not going to get anorexic because I can't be a fashion model,
don't worry. But don't tell me that appearance doesn't matter.
I'd believe in Santa Claus and the Easter Bunny before I'd believe that! Look, my body is something I deal with every day
at school, every time I go outside the house. Is it OK if I don't
have to deal with it at home?

Male Monologues

. . .

COMEDY

STYLE POINTS

(Looks in mirror, smooths hair, tweaks clothing.) Couple months ago, I started working on my style points. Know what I'm saying? Dressing a little better, a little more popular, paying attention to stuff like, figuring out you have to comb your hair in the morning — you don't get up and bust out into the world looking like you slept with your head in a blender set on frappé. And pretty soon, I see girls notice me, looking at me different than before, smiling even. And they notice I see them noticing. Which is way cool. Except now I have to figure out what to say when they want to talk!

JUST WIRED FUNNY

They say kids my age have problems getting enough rest. Something about a change in sleep-cycle rhythms. Here's a surefire cure. Have your parents ask you to cut the grass. You'll be comatose within seconds. Every time I'm supposed to cut the grass — or shovel snow or clean my room or sort clothes for washing — I feel the immediate and overwhelming need for a nap. I could have had fifteen Cokes in the last half hour, but somehow, all that sugar and caffeine reverses itself as soon as the prospect of extreme physical effort rears its ugly head, and my body cries out for sleep, hours of bountiful, blissful sleep! It's like my brain has an on-and-off switch. Work is mentioned, switch goes "Off!" Work goes away, switch goes back "On!" So you see, Mom and Dad, it's a scientific fact: I'm not lazy. I'm just wired funny.

FIRST KISS

There's this whole mystery about your first kiss. You know, what it's going to feel like when it happens with a girl you've thought about kissing for a while. I think it's going to taste like a cheeseburger medium well-done. OK, with maybe a thin layer of barbecue sauce in the middle to keep it rich and tender, light but filling with a tangy aftertaste depending on what lipstick she's using. And it's going to smell like the lighter fluid Dad uses to fire up the grill, sweet but fresh like an expensive brand of meat tenderizer. And inside — inside I'm going to feel like I'm blasting through space in a rocket to Mars. *(Closes eyes.)* Or maybe riding the baddest surfboard on the biggest wave in the ocean. There will be music — a whompin', stompin' head-banger by Papa Roach — and my whole body will be sizzling and chilling at the same time like I'm eating a giant jalapeno Klondike sandwich and suddenly, my heart will boil over and race pounding through my bloodstream till I nearly explode! And then I'll burp. *(Burps.)* Loudly. *(Burps more loudly.)* Wow! *(Opens eyes.)* Wonder what the second kiss is like?

DREAM JOB

When I was a little kid, my parents helped me put up a lemonade stand on our street. I don't remember selling much lemonade that day. Might have been because we ran out of lemon juice and used melted white cheese spread. But that gave me a taste for running my own business. And now that I'm on the verge of almost entering the minimum-wage teen work force, I've been thinking about my dream job: I'd like to work at a fireworks stand on the state highway. I'd be surrounded by hundreds of explosive devices slumbering peacefully in their cozy cardboard beds. Imagine the enormous concentration of propulsive power just snoozing under the rotting boards of that plywood shack! You'd meet lots of interesting people. Truck drivers and vagrants, maybe even real hobos with amazing life stories. And you'd test out some of the merchandise and shoot it off in the field behind the stand. Brrrwhaaaammmm! Sounds like a dream job to me!

TOO MUCH KNOWLEDGE . . .

Sometimes you can get more information about life than you really want. For instance, I drink about six Cokes a day to maintain my DMR of CLV — that's Daily Minimum Requirement of Carbonated Liquid Vitamins. Coke peps me up. Keeps me sharp, focused, alert, and always smiling. Until yesterday. That's when I saw an infomercial on TV where they used Coke to clean a really rancid toilet bowl. I mean, this bad boy had more layers of crust than a deep-dish pizza! I thought, "If Coke can eat through industrial-strength doo-doo, I wonder what it does to my stomach lining?" *(Shudders.)* Why is it the more I learn about life, the less I enjoy it?

PUT TOGETHER

(Standing in front of mirror, inspecting hair and face.) Big dance tonight. I've got to get put together. Let's see. I'll part my hair in the middle this time, yeah, like the drummer in Korn. Wish I had sideburns like the guy on *Smallville*. Or maybe Buffy's main dude, what's-his-name. Man, Wolverine really had some great chops in *X-Men*. Maybe the part should go over a little bit here, like the *Roswell* guy, the good alien, superbad. Sides look better, but, hey — what if I shaved my whole head! And left a top patch in the middle like that really crazy mother on *Celebrity Death Match*! Oh, wow, yeah, and then an earring in the right ear, a silver one with the cross just like the NBA all-star point guard wears — no, I got it — a rub-on tattoo of the new BioHazard CD cover on my forehead. Dude, you are so perfectly put together! That's what I like best about getting older: You finally can discover who you really are.

ACCORDION THERAPY

I've got a secret. Promise you won't tell a soul? If anyone found out, it would mean the end of my life as one of the cool kids in seventh grade. OK. *(Whispers into friend's ear.)* Oh, louder, OK. *(Loudly.)* I love my accordion. There, I said it! Ssshhh! Keep it down! I play drums with some guys in a little rock band, but you know what, I really love my accordion! I love the feel of it, the sound, the deep rumble of the chords, the high whine of the treble notes, the clack and clink of the keys. When I feel down, I just strap it on and start pushing back and forth, yeah, that's it, back and forth *(Mimes playing accordion.)*, get the wind going, just the drone, the deep, soothing power drone *(Hums a deep note.)* dummmmmmmmm . . . and then an octave above, dummmm . . . oh yeah, add a fifth to the bottom drone, dummm . . . dummm . . . bury yourself in the sound, sink into the drone, shape it with your body, float away in the magical mist of wheezy reeds — instant destressor! I think if more people had accordions — for therapy not for actual playing — there would be a lot less crazy stuff going on in the world. And accordion makers would be paid as much as psychiatrists!

SEA STORY

Gather round, lads and lassies, I'll tell you a tale of the Seven Seas! We were in the North Atlantic headed from Nantucket to Liverpool, when we hit the granddaddy of all storms. There were clouds and fog, and the sky got as black as balled pitch. Not a thing could be seen; why, the sun didn't come out for two weeks. When it did, we'd been blown up by the Gulf Stream and carried clear into the North Sea hard by Norway. The only way to get back to the Atlantic was through the English Channel, but it looked like our ship was too broad in the beam. I climbed up the rigging of the mainmast and looked ahead. On one side was France, the other England, with the steep, craggy Cliffs of Dover looming high overhead. I eyeballed the channel width and could see the ship was an inch narrower. It'll be a tight squeeze, says I, so I ordered the crew to soap the sides so she could squeeze through easylike, a mite more on the starboard side, soaped up and down till the ship was slick as glass! Well, we cast off, and when we hit the Channel, she squeaked and scraped, and all the soap on the starboard rubbed off on the Dover side, but we made it with nary an inch to spare. And that's why the Cliffs of Dover are white to this very day!

Male Monologues

• • •

DRAMA

JOHN HENRY WAS A NATURAL MAN

This is the story of a great American hero, John Henry. You all heard of John Henry! He was a natural man. He could drill more holes and drill 'em deeper than any other man on the railroad. Drill the holes, dynamite goes in — *blammity-wham-blam!* Tunnel comes through. That's because John Henry was a natural man. Had a hammer in each hand and a mouthful of spikes. He'd spit out the spikes — *thew! thew!* — and swing those hammers down — *whop! whop!* — and pound down those ties just ahead of a steaming train.

One day a salesman came up to the track boss and tried to sell him a steam drill. Boss said, "I got a man here, a natural man named John Henry, can beat that steam drill every time." Salesman and the boss placed a bet. Salesman said, "No man can beat a machine!" John Henry said, "He can if he's a natural man!"

Well, the drill started up, and the drill kept on turning. Sweet Polly Ann, John Henry's wife, she said, "John Henry, that hammer will be the death of you!" *(Mimes motions with hammers.)* But John Henry, he kept on driving — *whop!* — kept on driving into that rock-hard mountain — *whop!* — sun went high in the sky — *whop!* — sun went low in the sky — *whop!* — steam drill kept on turning, John Henry kept on driving — *whop!* — before he'd let that steam drill beat him down, he'd die with his hammer in his hand — *whop!* — till all of a sudden John Henry broke through the rock and had twice as many holes drilled cleaner and deeper than that steam drill! Yes, ma'am, he beat that machine, beat it because he was a natural man!

SHORT END OF THE STICK

Brian Mitchell was a kid in my summer camp last year. Meanness seemed to hang over him like a cloud. He made enemies faster than a tire makes tracks in mud. So it wasn't much of a surprise when the last night, some kids snuck into camp with knives and ropes and BB guns. They weren't going to just scare Brian Mitchell. They were going to hurt him.

I was almost asleep when there was a hideous bunch of screams. Like wolves howling after prey. The guy next to me said, "All the counselors are at the lodge across the lake." A guy in the other bunk said, "He'll be hanging from a tree in twenty minutes. Anybody wanna bet on it?" Another howl. They were hunting Brian Mitchell like an animal.

Now, you never knew my dad before he died, but when it came to standing up for his family or an individual getting the short end of the stick, you couldn't budge him with a bulldozer. "Son," he'd say, "you'll meet bullies all your life. Some even that wear nice suits and act like they own the world. When you see them bullying somebody weaker and getting away with it because they're bigger or richer, you gotta squawk. I'm not saying be a crybaby. I'm saying, you stand up and say straight out, it ain't right and shouldn't be allowed. You squawk." I hated when he talked to me like that. Babies squawk. Chickens squawk. I'd think of a diapered baby with a chicken head running in circles squawk-squawk-squawking every time I heard the word.

A BB-gun shot and then shouts came from near the mess hall. I figured Brian was making for the camp entrance by the highway. He'd have to fight through a deep tangled ravine with no trails, then cross an open field where he'd be easily spotted in the moonlight. Or he might blunder into the sinkhole marsh we'd been warned to keep away from. But if the counselors knew, they could drive down the east trail and intercept the chase.

I can't say why I dressed and slipped out of the tent. Maybe it was raw excitement. Maybe it was morbid curiosity. But as I ran through the dark woods — mixed in with the screams and the shots, I could hear something else — my dad's cancer-ravaged voice urging me on: "It ain't right and shouldn't be allowed."

I WANTED TO PLAY

(Winding up, practicing a baseball pitch.) Tomorrow is the last game of the season. If we win, we go to finals. And it's my turn to pitch. *(Throws.)* Well, it was until today. Coach says he's going to start Mickey Dobson, even though the whole summer, I've been a starter. Take my turn every fourth game, the way they do it in the big leagues. Guess I'm pretty good, or I'd be playing shortstop, which is where I was last year. *(Pounds ball into mitt.)* Coach says Mickey's better against lefties, which is not true. But if Mickey pitches, Coach's son, Josh, gets to play centerfield and gets a chance to get one more hit and win the batting title. And win a digital camera from the team sponsor, Photo Maxx. Which my aunt says buys stuff from Coach's advertising business, whatever. *(Goes into windup, stares intensely at home plate, then sighs and relaxes.)* I joined Little League 'cause I wanted to play baseball. I didn't do it to play *games*. That's for grown-ups.

THE UNITED STATES OF BUTT-KICK

Just heard the results of the new survey on school violence. Schools are safer than ever before, it says. Violence is down nationwide. Uh-huh. Guess the kids in this school didn't see that survey. Or maybe they live in a different nation, the United States of Butt-Kick. *(Shows top of head.)* See that? Thirty-three stitches from some eighth grader who smacked me on the head with a metal stool 'cause I looked like some guy on TV he didn't like. Or maybe it was a racial thing. Or maybe he's just on the wrong medication. Who knows? I was unconscious, and I don't think he stuck around to answer any survey questions.

HALF-AND-HALF

It's no big deal being so-called mixed race. I don't think I've ever had someone not serve me at a restaurant or beat me up 'cause I'm half-and-half. White kids try extra hard to show how cool they are by ignoring the race thing. And the only time black kids get weird is when the actual subject of race comes up. Like these rap songs always talking about there's going to be a race war. That sells records and gets headlines on the news for the bammer-of-the-month. But my black friends, they'll say, "Hey, what side you gonna be on when it start to ball up? Yeah, dawg, gonna be a big grillin', off da hinges. Woulda told you about it, but, you know, you're half-and-half, homies don't know if you can be trusted." Trusted. To do what? Be a whole dummy half the time?

A BIG RESPONSIBILITY

All right! Let's go! *(Waves a group forward.)* Hey, guys! See you at recess! *(Steps to one side and addresses audience.)* I've been a school crossing guard for about two weeks, and I really like it! It's a big responsibility, my dad says. Plus you get to wear this badge and a special jacket with a wicked logo of a lightning bolt and a pair of feet with wings. And you get to skip the first fifteen minutes of home room and leave last period fifteen minutes early. All you do is wait for the WALK light and help kids cross the street, but — I don't know . . . I just found out the guard at Kessler takes money from the first graders. He tells them it's a "crossing fee," and they have to pay him or he doesn't let them cross. All the other guards do it, he says. A bonus, he says. I bet if I asked the principal, I'd find out it wasn't a bonus. *(Sighs.)* This is a busy street, and I really like helping kids cross. But being a snitch . . . *(Touches badge reverently.)* I guess doing things you don't like is a responsibility, too.

BROTHERS UNTIL DEATH

I didn't think it would be any big deal to show Jimmy how to huff. He's my little brother, *y que*, what you gonna do about it? I figured he'd get so sick he'd quit following me and my friends around. But Jimmy wanted to be part of *la clica* — *carnalitos hasta la muerta*, brothers to the death. When we weren't around, he got some solvent from our dad's garage. And to show how *malo loco* he was, he tied a plastic bag around his head to get a bigger jack. Jimmy took a deep breath straight from the can and passed out . . . he'll never come out of *la coma*. Now my parents ask, why? Why would he want to do something like this? What vile person taught him something so stupid and so destructive? I can't tell them . . . I can't tell them it was me, his *carnal* . . . his brother to the death.

A LIFE LIKE THIS

Yes, I have heard the jokes. You know your Amish preteen is in trouble when they stay in bed after six A.M. Or, An Amish drunk driver was recently pulled over for trotting under the influence of cottage cheese. Yes, I find them funny, too. And sometimes I do wish I were going to school past eighth grade like my non-Amish friends. Sometimes I wish I could pick up a telephone or turn on a light switch, watch TV or go to a movie. I see the world out there, and I know there's so much of it I won't ever know or do living on this farm, in this small town, with these people. But — look at that fence. *(Points.)* I just built it, my dad and I. And that calf over there. I helped when it was born, and I'll help when it dies to feed our family. Amish kids see reality at a different level than you think. We see it more up close, 'cause we have fewer distractions. I can always join the world outside here. But people out there, they might live their whole lives and never know they could have a life like this.

PARTY TIME

(Talking on phone.) Yeah, sounds phat! I'm down wid it! Straight up! Peace out! *(Clicks off.)* Party at Vanessa's house tonight. Her parents are gone for the weekend. *(Frowns.)* I'm not sure I really want to go. Sure, I *want* to go, 'cause it's a party, and everybody's gonna be there, everybody that's Type Hot! But everybody is gonna be drinking and smoking, getting pretty baked. And there's couples hooking up right in the open, and I heard last time there was a girl in her underwear, you know, dancing. Parties like that look cool when you see them in a movie. But when you're right in the middle of one, you feel like you don't belong. I dunno. I feel weird enough doing normal things. I'm not sure I want to go to a party and feel weirder still.

SENSE OF ACCOMPLISHMENT

Here's all you need. Binoculars, putty knife, two slim jims, a hammer and screwdriver. You're set. Naw, I've done this a hundred times. It's a snap. You watch awhile, make sure nobody's home, find the right door or window, then, bam! — showtime, you're in, you're out. I dunno. Some guys go for cash and credit cards, jewels and stuff. Some go for electronics, whatever you can carry. Me? I never take anything. Really. My parents both make like a hundred grand a year, I don't need to pawn Game Boys for pocket money. Didn't you see all the crap they got me for my birthday? Jeez, it looks like they bought out the whole first floor at Circuit City! Naw, I don't rack for money. I do it for the sense of accomplishment. That's something my parents can't just go out and buy me.

Female/Male Monologues

· · ·

COMEDY

"PRE" *THIS!*

Can someone tell me what's with this "pre" teen stuff? It's like training wheels for being a teenager. Like you can't quite be trusted with being an actual teenager — as if that exalted state of humanhood required some kind of advanced degree! Preteens also get labeled as prepubescent and preadolescent. Yeah, uh-huh, keep rubbing it in, keep ratcheting up our hormonally induced sense of inferiority, why not just say we're prehuman while you're at it? But don't forget we're also precocious, precipitous, preconscious and prematurely predisposed to pretend we're presumably and preposterously precarious and prehensile. And it's all predestined! So, hey, world: pre *this!* *(Throws out arms.)*

QUORUM

Yo, people! Now that we have a quorum, maybe we should get down to business. All rise! The six hundred and twenty-ninth secret meeting of the Mighty Marvel Milk Dud Avengers is called to order.

Flubadub-rubadub tinka-tonka hee-haw!
Winky-dink kitchen-sink cowabunga seesaw!
Do-re-mi-fa-so-la-ti!
Don't sit on a bumblebee!
Milkkkkkkkkk Dud!
(Pat head.) Yabba-dabba-doo-dog!
(Stamp feet twice.) Dum-dum, dum-dum!
(Wrench shoulders back twice.) Ow-oooo-ga! Ow-oooo-ga!
(Leap in the air.) Milk Duds!

(Stand at attention, hand over heart.) I pledge allegiance to the Milk Duds, and to the chocolate goodness for which they stand. One candy, indivisible and chewy over all, so help my cavities, amen.

Mighty!
Marvel!
Milk Dud!
Avengers!
Rule!
Forever!

Can we skip the secret handshake? *(Rub left arm.)* I think I got poison ivy.

MY GOALS

I didn't have a single goal until I was nine and a half. Then I got one — just a little, teeny practice goal. Which was to sample every flavor of ice cream that existed in the entire world. My life was transformed. I had direction! I had purpose! I had a goal! Now, some people might tell you that's not much of a goal. Sampling every ice cream flavor in the world doesn't improve *anything*. It doesn't help *anybody*. It may even be a complete *waste* of time and effort. But it did teach me one very important lesson that will certainly shape my growth into a mature adult — I really, really, really *like* ice cream!

SUMMER SURE GOES FAST

Summer sure goes fast when you're this age. We went to a state park for vacation. It was cool until my big brother ran into a bear. Got away, though. Lucky for the bear! So we came home and my Aunt Sally had her special meatloaf recipe printed in the newspaper. Then her oven caught fire, and her kitchen burned. Then she started dating one of the firemen, and they got married last week. It was a strange summer. Things came and went and then came back again. My mom's computer crashed. Then it got stolen from the repair shop. So the insurance bought a new computer she uses to do her job from home, and she makes more money than before. So we went to the state park for another vacation. This time my big brother ran into a waterfall. He survived and got to be on *America's Dumbest Injury Videos*. That's where the studio people saw me and asked if I wanted to be in the next *Star Wars* movie. It was a strange summer. After we finish filming, I can hardly wait for it to start over again.

RIDDLE-MANIA

OK, people, it's time for Riddle-Mania! Arrrrrrrre you ready? Why did the gum cross the road? Because it was stuck to the chicken's foot!

Then why did the elephant cross the road? Because he was tied to the chicken! So why did the rooster cross the road? Because the chicken was on vacation! *(Giggles.)*

Of course, you know that the first great riddle was from the theater. In *Oedipus Rex* by Sophocles, the Sphinx asks: "Who in infancy walks on four legs, in middle age on two, in old age on three?" Oedipus replies: "Man — who as a baby crawls on all fours, as an adult walks on two legs, and as a senior citizen leans on a cane." He didn't say anything about those electric golf cart thingies old folks ride around in these days, but, hey, Oedipus wasn't exactly the brightest bulb in the bean patch, seeing as how he poked out his own eyes — talk about a klutz! *(Points skyward, above left.)* Wow, looks like a storm is coming. *(To audience.)* When is a storm cloud not fully dressed? When it's only wearing thunder wear! *(Laughs.)*

A MORE STABLE CAREER

My middle school isn't ranked very high on the educational pyramid. Our chemistry teacher thinks the melting point of cadmium is the temperature of a Cadillac engine. Our history teacher told us that not only did Christopher Columbus discover America, he invented the first electric pizza maker. But I am going to overcome these obstacles and study hard and someday win a scholarship to M.I.T. Right, the Mary Kay Institute of Tupperware. Of course I'm talking about the Massachusetts Institute of Technology! I will major in nuclear physics and join the elite team of rocket scientists working on the space program. But my counselor says I should think about a more stable career. Something in heavy metals — like body piercing.

WONDER YEARS

My parents always say these are my Wonder Years. I have no idea what they're talking about — something to do with bread and twelve different ways of bodybuilding. Who knows about parents? They live in their own universe! But every now and then, I do wonder . . . Are there really twenty-four hours in a day? Or are there more and somebody has been hiding them somewhere just so I have to get up earlier? And I wonder if animals really do understand human language and think we're all dumber than rocks. I wonder how long it really takes for paint to dry if you sit and watch it. I wonder if fishermen are able to make a living from their net income. I wonder if you'd get fired from a sandwich shop if you couldn't cut the mustard. I wonder why it seems no one is listening until you say something really dumb. I wonder if I'll get this part. I wonder if I'll spend my whole life asking questions with no answers. I guess my parents are right. These are my Wonder Years. I wonder how they knew that?

BIRTHDAY BASH

(Sings last line of "Happy Birthday.") "Happy birthday to you!" *(Claps.)* Oh, yeah, I like birthdays! I like birthdays so much that when I was seven, I woke up every morning pretending I had a new name, which meant I was a new person and it was *this* person's birthday! Couldn't get my parents to buy into it. Might have been the part about wanting Mom to make a fresh birthday cake every day. But isn't there something really awesome about celebrating a birthday? It's the best day a kid's going to have all year, and it's all about you! I started thinking: If you *could* celebrate a birthday every day, life would be unbelievably cool! So every Saturday I come here, to this nursing home, and help put on a birthday party. Somebody always has a birthday that week or the week coming up, or someone in their family had one or might have one, whatever! They serve cake and ice cream and soda and somebody sings a song or tells a funny story, and I learned how to do a couple of magic tricks just to keep everybody awake, and sometimes I bring a couple of friends and they sing and dance, and let's face it — a lot of these older folks, they're a lot like you and me — they don't mind having as much free fun as often as they can, without any parents around!

Hey, here's a new birthday song* I made up! Sing along! *(Sings.)*

> Your birthday is a very special day
> Full of fun and friends and so many games to play.
> We wish you lots of happiness and cheer
> Because your birthday is the best day of the year.

*Music score for this song can be found on page 123.

THERE WENT MY ELECTRODES

Remote-controlled rats. Sounds like the name of one of my brother's favorite rock bands, but no — it's for real, sort of. I just read where scientists have implanted electrodes in the brain of a rat. They can make the rat turn left and right, climb up and down, maybe even tap dance and do algebra. I think people are wondering, "If they can do this with rats, can they do it to humans?" I'm wondering, maybe they already *have*. Haven't you ever been walking along minding your own business, thinking, say, about the table of periodic elements — when, suddenly, you hear a candy bar calling your name? You turn and walk miles and miles and miles until you find a store that sells that exact candy bar. Then you realize buying the candy bar will almost use up the exact amount of money your parents gave you to get a roll of paper towels to clean up all that spilled milk from breakfast. Bzzzzip! *(Jerks head to side.)* Your electrode kicks in and you realize you cannot eat the candy bar without fruit juice — Bzzzzip! *(Jerks head.)* — you turn and spend almost your last dollar on the juice — Bzzzzip! *(Jerks head.)* — a repast that cannot be consumed until purchasing with the very last few cents remaining in your pocket the latest issue of *Cool Preteen Stuff for Cool Preteens. (Pause.)* I think this may explain a lot of what parents call "immature behavior" in young people. Bzzzzip! *(Jerks head, whole body.)* Ooops, there went my electrodes! Gotta go!

DON'T CALL ME LEFTY

I am not a backward person! But, being a left-hander, I am forced to live in a righty-tighty, lefty-loosey world. A world of intrinsic bias where each and every object conspires to resist and humiliate me. That would include your basic corkscrew, can opener, juice squeezer, computer keyboard, drill press, band saw, doorknob, and scissors. Not to mention, thank you very much, your garden variety golf club and guitar, and let's also not forget industrial meat slicers and the big iron lever you pull when you want to yank open a trap door and send somebody plummeting to their eternal doom. *All* of which I may very well *want* to use at some point in my life. Especially the eternal doom thing for the next person who tries to give me a left-handed compliment!

JUST FOR THE HECK OF IT

Sometimes I look at older people like my parents, and I worry. Not about them, about me! About *me* growing up and becoming like *them*, which is to say, totally losing the ability to be spontaneous. Spur of the moment. Off the cuff. Wild and crazy. Like jumping into a stream with your clothes on. Running barefoot in the snow. Puddle-stomping in the rain. Rolling around in the grass and babbling *babba-da babba-da babba-da* nonsense talk till you break out laughing for an hour. I know that when you grow up you have a lot of responsibility, but it seems like you also have a lot more power. The power to get a cool job and earn lots of money and live and travel anywhere you want. All I want when I grow up is one power — the power to do something just for the heck of it.

YES, I AM A GENIUS

I sometimes think I am a kind of genius with a real gift. Some days it's a gift for painting. Other days for dancing. Yesterday it was for designing video games. Today it's for playing three-dimensional chess, and tomorrow — who knows? I guess the reason I think I'm a genius is because when I do something I feel like it is the most important thing in the world to do. I feel like it is the *only* thing in the world I want to do — ever — for the rest of my life. But people laugh and say, "Oh, you'll grow out of it. It's just a phase." But what if I don't? What if I'm like a plant just trying to live and grow but not getting sun and water and then shriveling and dying and disappearing into nothing? I wonder if when you grow up and people know you're a genius, they let you be one . . .

TONGUE TWISTER

Hewo . . . jus gah mah tongue pierce . . . hurd a liddle . . . look priddy, huh? *(Opens mouth, grimaces.)* Oww! Mah parens gonna be surprise . . . They thoughd I was gonna ged a new pair shoes, ha-ha-ha — *(Laughs, then grimaces.)* Oww! Only hurds when I laugh, ha-ha-ha — *(Laughs, then grimaces.)* Oww! Wanna know real reason I gah mah tongue pierce? I dond wanna wear braces . . . make me talk funny! Ha-ha-ha — *(Laughs, then grimaces.)* Oww!

SO, WHAT'S UP WITH WIND?

I am not a big fan of wind. You know, the thing that makes the air seem colder and blows stuff in your face — snow in the winter, rain in the summer — and always messes up your hair and snarls your clothes and makes everything just a big, whipping, flying-around mess. What's up with wind, anyway? Why did God put it into the world? So it moves plant seeds from Point A to Point B to fertilize things; OK, don't they have city workers for that? Excuse me? The wind moves the weather from place to place. Well, why can't it take a plane or cruise ship? Just load the weather up and cart it around so everybody gets the right amount of weather they need when they want it. Like a satellite TV channel, you get the weather you order. Of course, if you fell behind on your payments, I guess they'd just cancel your weather. Well, at least you wouldn't have any messy wind.

CAREER DAY

They had a career day at our middle school last week. They said we were never too young to start thinking about a career. Well, the first thing I thought of about a career is what kind of word is *career*, anyway? Apparently, it comes from an old Latin word that meant *road*. OK, a career is a road. They both take you someplace. Awesome, I'm down with that. But do you have to know *where* you want to go? Can you have a career — not a road-type career that takes you someplace — but a career that takes you someplace you just don't exactly know where? In other words, can I have a career just standing here like I am now doing what I'm doing now, which is thinking about stuff and talking to people about it? 'Cause that's the career I'm really looking for: I talk, you listen, you pay me money and do what I say. Hmmm, maybe they have a job like that already. It's called middle school principal.

I'M NOT STRESSED

They say preteens are getting more stressed these days. I don't know why, 'cause I'm not stressed. After school I have a relaxing tennis lesson that gets out any stress from the day's class work. That's on Monday at 3:30. Then at five, I do jazz dance, and that really loosens me up for a good dinner at six. Then at 7:30 I practice violin for an hour — music really mellows me out — and I'm ready to dig into three or four hours of homework, except that this Monday I'll have to get that finished up a little quicker 'cause I'm doing an online interview with the school paper at nine. Did I tell you, I'm running for Student Council? Which would fit great in my Tuesday schedule, since I have an open hour between 4-H at six o'clock and Sixth Grade Knowledge Bowl at four — no, wait, I think it's Sixth Grade Knowledge Bowl at six and 4-H at four — no, that's not right, because tae-bo is Tuesday and soccer is Saturday, which means — or is it tae-bo Saturday, soccer Tuesday, S and S, T and T? Let's see, if Students Against Underachieving is Friday at one, then Honor Band is Wednesday at five, which means science club is, huh-huh-huh — *(Begins stuttering, quivering.)* no-no, tennis tournament is Tuesday, oh no, did I miss practice! Huh-huh-huh — impossible! Then where did that hour go? I've lost an hour! No! An hour without activity, no! An hour without structure, no! An hour without a goal I can win a prize for, nooooo! *(Pause, calming.)* You're right. I need to simplify my life. Got it! I'll sign up for Stress Busters Club! I think they just started one at church. If they didn't, then I'll start one. And run for president. No, too much stress. I'll just be activities director. I'm really good at scheduling!

MOVING TARGET

(Ducks as if being shot at.) Whoa! Almost got me that time! *(Rises warily.)* It's not easy being a target every minute of your life, hunted like prey — by advertisers! To them, preteens are the most highly prized catch in the demographic jungle. They stalk us mercilessly, day and night, targeting us with the most diabolical product messages you can imagine — on radio and TV, at the mall and school, even in our textbooks! *(Ducks.)* Watch out! It's a soft drink ad aimed right at your vulnerable self-esteem! *(Rises warily.)* Business spends over a hundred fifty billion dollars a year targeting preteens. Then you're captured and name-branded for the rest of your life! My name is not Calvin! My name is not FUBU! I will not be a slave to Tommy or Victoria or the nefarious Billabong! I am a human being, not a consumer! I will live free and untrendy! I — aaahhh! *(Staggers as if shot, grabs ankle.)* They got me in the Reeboks . . . with a Blazing McNugget!

SILENCE OF THE FOLLICLES

Ssssh! Listen. Can you hear it? Ssssh! There it is! It's the sound of your hair. Growing. Out from your head, millimeter by creeping millimeter. Inside your head, pushing up from your skull through the skin. Breaking through the skin, several layers of skin — krrgghhhhhhh! — erupting like little barbed spears, even the finest strands, crunching through the crackling skin — pakrrgghhh! — there's one! — pakrrgghhh! there's another! — pakrrgghhh! pakrrgghhh! pakrrgghhh! — thousands of them every second crunching and smashing and ripping and tearing, swarming all over your head devouring your scalp! Unstoppable! Invincible! And then there's the silence . . . the silence of the follicles . . . regrouping, waiting to make their next move, waiting to push forth . . . and sprout. *(Cackles with diabolical laughter.)* You think listening to your hair *grow* is scary? Wait till you go get your hair *cut!*

AQUA VIVA

(Bending over, peering into a fish tank.) Wouldn't it be wild to live in a fish tank? I mean, to be a *fish* living in a fish tank. You'd always get to swim whenever you wanted. Free snacks to nibble on any time of day or night. And you'd get to know pretty much everything there was to know about your whole world. You wouldn't have to go to school. No classes, no grades, no cliques or clubs you couldn't belong to. No parents losing their jobs and getting divorced and you having to move to some stupid town you don't like where nobody likes you. No worrying about what high school's going to be like or if you'll be smart enough to get into college or if anybody *ever* is going to go out with you on a date — nope, if you were living in that fish tank right there, life would be pretty simple. And wet.

COMPUTO, ERGO ME AMO

(Stands zombielike.) I am blind. I am deaf. I am mute. *(Shouts.)* Yes, mute! My computer is down, and it's like every sense has been stripped away! I can't e-mail, can't instant message. Can't J-peg or Quicktime. Can't PDF or scan. It's like my thumbs have been cut off at the knees! Computo, ergo me amo. Without a computer I cease to exist as a functional human! Please, please, pleasssssse, Mom, can we get this hard drive defragged before I dematerialize! What's this? A book? *(Recoils.)* You have to touch it? *(Sniffs.)* Smells like paper! And it feels so, so papery! Well, I guess I can use it until the computer's fixed. Next thing you know, I'll be reduced to eating food that hasn't been grown in a microwave.

TOP TEN WARNING SIGNS OF PRE-TEEN SUICIDE

Here are the Top Ten Warning Signs of Preteen Suicide:

One, I hate you. Two, I hate you. Three, I hate you. Four, I hate you. Five — OK, just kidding. But seriously, *this* is what parents need to look for to prevent their preteen from killing him and/or herself.

One. I clean my room without you nagging for hours.

Two. I accept responsibility for my mistakes and take blame for things that aren't my fault, like global warming and badly written teen sitcoms.

Three. I exhibit severe hallucinations and tell you how great I think my teachers are.

Four. I gets lots of sleep and don't argue with you about staying up all night.

Five. Massive change in appetite — I no longer consume fifteen pounds of processed sugar a day but occasionally eat a green vegetable. Or three, if served with ketchup.

Six. Loss of interest in hobbies — I've stopped spending eight hours a night playing video games.

Seven. Major mood changes — I appear at breakfast with a smile and call my sister a "pencil-neck freakazoid" no more than once a day.

Eight. Giving away prized possessions — I sell my Kurt, Janis, Sid, and Elvis Celebrity Death Dolls on eBay and put the money in a college savings fund.

Nine. Running away from home — I spend weekends at the library tutoring second-graders.

And the tenth most ominous warning sign of preteen suicide — rebellious statements intended to shock: "Mom and Dad, I love you!"

What? These are signs of maturity not dysfunction? Oh no! I've turned into a grown-up! Quick, somebody kill me, please!

OLD ENOUGH

(*Rapturously.*) I am in love! But my parents, naturally, they're opposed. "Too young," they say. "Not ready emotionally. You'll just end up getting hurt." Look, I know it's a big step. I know it's going to demand incredible commitment and maturity. Yes, I know I'm only eleven years old, but in some societies, that *is* old enough! Look, it's *my* life we're talking about here. *My* growth, *my* needs, you can't keep us apart, it's *destiny!* Mom, Dad — I've got to have a cell phone!

HAPPY HOLIDAZE

What about my report card? Excessive Unexcused Absences? I beg to differ! They were all holidays. All seventy-four of them. Our teacher said celebrating holidays shows respect for traditions of all people; that's a good thing, right? And nobody goes to school on a holiday! Not on Chinese New Year or Scottish New Year's Bank Holiday! Or on Benjamin Franklin's Birthday, National School Nurse Day, Professional Secretaries Day, or the Grand Duchess' Birthday in Luxembourg. And there was Errol Barrow Day in Barbados, Waitangi Day in New Zealand, St. Lucia Day in Italy and Sweden, Guadalupe Day and Cinco De Mayo in Mexico, Shichi-Go-San — that's Seven-Five-Three Day — in Japan. Lots and lots of English holidays: Guy Fawkes Day, Boxing Day, Queen Mum's Birthday, Mothering Sunday — which, of course, you have to celebrate on the preceding Friday and following Monday. And not to forget one of the biggest excused holidays of all: the start of International Healthy Weight Awareness Week, also known as Johnny Weismuller Swimming 100 Meters in Less Than One Minute Day. So, you can see how much I learned from *not* being at school this semester. I think that calls for a special holiday, don't you?

MY ANGER JOURNAL

The school counselor says I'm supposed to keep an Anger Journal. Whenever you start to feel angry about something — or somebody, usually, like the school counselor — you stop and write down what you're angry about and why. *(Sighs.)* OK, here goes. *(Writes.)* I am angry at having to keep a quote-unquote anger journal. I am angry that I can't just be angry 'cause I feel like being angry. I am angry that I am wasting quality anger time on merely writing about anger, when I could be doing some of my favorite anger activities such as yelling, stomping, raging, and seething. I am angry that I have to explain and defend my anger. It should be obvious: I am angry because I choose to be, and because I am very, *very* good at it. I am angry that when I write about anger, no one can actually see me being angry. Who wants to read about somebody's dumb old anger when they could have seen it for real and been majorly entertained? Borrrrr-ing! I mean — that's weird . . . now I can't remember what I was angry about in the first place. Hey, this anger journal stuff really works. *(Clenches fists, shouts.)* And *that* makes me *really* angry!

SECRET POWER

I'm not so worried about starting a new school this fall. I think I can handle it. Well, I *dreamed* I can handle it. Last night I dreamed I was eating in a restaurant with my dog, Picasso. I was having spaghetti and pancakes, and Picasso was having pork chops with macaroni, and this restaurant was at the top of a very tall building, two hundred stories high! The view was awesome, you could see all the way to Paris and London and even the North Pole, but then Picasso saw a bird go by and jumped off the balcony! He was going to fall two hundred stories! But instead of screaming or crying for Dad or hiding under the table, I shouted, "Wind! Wind! Wind!," and I ordered the wind to blow him back up to the balcony. I believed with all my heart that I could will the wind to change direction and blow him back. "Wind! Wind! Wind!" And a big gust of wind blew Picasso back up as he was falling and right back into my arms! Oh ho, yes! It was like I had this secret power inside me all the time to make bad things turn out good. I just had to concentrate and have faith and will the good thing to happen. Oh, yeah, I am ready for school! *(Pause.)* You know what's really weird about that dream? I don't have a dog named Picasso. Heck, in real life, I don't even have a dog.

WORLDLY KNOWLEDGE

I've just finished my first year of middle school. According to my report card, I didn't get very high grades. As if mere grades could measure the true extent of my knowledge about the world! Hah! Middle school won't tell you the way things really work in the universe. It won't tell you there are forty-four million ways to make bingo on a single bingo card. It won't tell you that rubber bands last longer when refrigerated. Or a shark is the only fish that can blink with both eyes. That there are more chickens than people in the world, that a cat has thirty-two muscles in each ear, mosquitoes are more likely to bite if you've just eaten a banana, and you won't get new freckles after you're twenty. Middle school never dared to tell me that elephants have four knees, an ostrich eye is bigger than its brain, and a sneeze travels from your mouth at over one hundred miles an hour. And, believe me, people, middle school doesn't *want* you to know that a dragonfly has a life span of twenty-four hours, a goldfish a memory span of three seconds, and the average grown-up laughs fifteen times a day, the average kid, four hundred. Start laughing now, folks, 'cause in two seconds I'm going to forget everything I learned in school this year — including this!

HOTLINE

(Answers phone.) Hello, you've reached the Hotline Hotline. The Hotline Hotline is a 24-hour service where you can talk to a real person about a problem for which there is no actual hotline, or because you just need to think you have a problem and want to talk about it with someone you believe is actually listening. The Hotline Hotline provides no referrals, counseling, or any useful information whatever — unless babbling into the ear of a complete stranger is your idea of useful. But we'll listen to you anyway because it's a lonnnnnnng, slow Saturday night, and the Stuck-At-Home-Alone-Babysitting-Your-Baby-Brother-and-Sister Hotline is closed for the weekend. Have a nice day! *(Hangs up.)*

SOME IMAGINATION

You know the worst thing about being a kid? Having grown-ups tell you tall tales and thinking you believe them. My mom says that when she was my age, instead of cell phones, people used to have to talk on something called a *party line*, which sounds cool until you realize everybody in the whole town was listening in on your call — especially some nosy busybody named Ma Bell. Then there were *milkmen* that left milk bottles on your doorstep at night. Really, and they were filled with milk! And there was a guy called the Fuller Brush Man who roamed the neighborhoods selling stuff for your bathroom. How weird is that? And she said they had candy cigarettes but no computers and no Diet Coke. And McDonald's hamburgers were fifteen cents and MTV used to have music instead of game shows. Unreal! Next she'll be telling me televisions came with only thirteen channels and no remote!

EVERYBODY SING!

Oh no, please no. Please, don't let it happen! Not here, not now, not again! *(Buries head in hands, looks up terrified.)* Indescribable agony. A recurring nightmare, over and over. It starts like this: I'm riding in the car with a new friend, somebody I really want to make major prop points with. Suddenly, like a fire-drill siren, my dad starts singing! Some prehistoric oldies tune with idiotic lyrics like "I am the walrus!" or "Doo-wah-diddy-diddy-dum-diddy-doo!" or "Girls Just Wanna Have Fu-uuunnnn." And there's no escape. If I try to talk over him, he thinks I'm joining in and just sings louder. I turn to my friend, roll my eyes, give a goofy grin. Maybe they play along and giggle. But sometimes, the horror is too much, and they stare out the window, glassy-eyed, frozen with shock. Dad, I really appreciate you being chauffeur guy. But if I pay for gas, will you promise to, like, pretend you've had a vocal lobotomy?

THINGS I'VE LEARNED
AS A PRETEEN

Things I've learned about life since becoming a preteen: If you squirt hair spray on dust bunnies and run over them with roller blades, they *will* catch fire. Just when I get my room the way I like it, Mom makes me clean it up. Super glue is forever. It's way more fun to color *outside* the lines. Even Popeye didn't eat his spinach until he absolutely had to. There is no good reason why clothes have to match. I'm always anxious to test the water, until I find out it's really cold. Garbage bags do not make good parachutes. More important, I've learned no matter how much Jell-O you put in a swimming pool, you still can't walk on water. I've learned I like my teacher 'cause he cries when we sing "Come All Ye Faithful." And that if you want a kitten, start out asking for a horse. And though it's hard to admit, I'm secretly glad my parents are strict with me. But most important of all, I've learned that if you want to cheer yourself up, you should try cheering up someone else first. And I've learned that the world is a funny place, but not enough people are laughing. And that when you've been fishing for six hours and haven't caught anything except poison ivy and a sunburn, you're still better off than the worm at the end of your hook.

CIVIL DISOBEDIENCE

Yes, officer, my villainous crime of feeding the ducks is the fault of my parents. They taught me my ABC's, which in turn, led to my learning to read. And then they put a fully loaded library card in my childish hands, a weapon I used with full premeditated intent to peruse the works of one Henry David Thoreau. You know, the civil disobedience guy who said that when unjust laws exist, you've got three choices: one, obey them; two, obey them while working to change them; and three, stop obeying them at once. Honestly, officer, I went with choice number three, 'cause I don't care what the stupid sign says — I'm feeding the ducks at the park. I'm going to feed them until you pry the last, measly bread crumb from my cold, dead fingers. I'm going to feed ducks no matter how many times you say you're going to arrest me, because it's the right thing to do to help hungry animals. Or as Thoreau would say, "That government is best which feeds ducks the most!"

Z-TOWN BLUES

(Head down, asleep, waking up with a start.) Ummm, whaaa, no, Miss Hansen, I wasn't sleeping, no, I was, ummm, trying to pick up a contact lens without using my hands. Ummm, actually, I was *(Stifles yawn.)* testing the desk for drool resistance, it's a project for science class. *(Stifles bigger yawn.)* Beg pardon? I agree, a short power nap is one of the seven habits of highly defective people, and sleeping in class, well, it's sort of like working smarter, not harder, isn't it? Not that I was *(Stifles even bigger yawn.)* sleeping, just expanding the brain circuits through deep, deep . . . *(Yawns.)* deeeeeppp. . . *(Nods off, snores loudly, awakes with a start, and shouts.)* Bingo!

CASE IN POINT

I don't know how my parents ever survived this long in the cruel, harsh laboratory of life. Case in point: I got grounded last week for breaking curfew. So last night I snuck out and went to my best friend's house to watch *The OC*. Naturally, I got busted and double-grounded. And then triple-grounded! The reason for this cruel and unusual max detention? *(Parental voice.)* "You didn't leave a note telling us where you went." Hold on to your space hats, junior rocketeers — my parents actually expected me to leave a note saying I was going out when I was grounded in the first place? That's like, you're going to cheat on a test, so you tell the teacher, "Excuse me, would you please look the other way so I can peek at my friend's paper?" *(Chuckles.)* Parents . . . such innocents! When will they ever learn?

ALWAYS THE GIGGLING

I really get yucked out when I see my parents kissing. It's grotesque! No, not kissing each *other* . . . kissing their new lovers! After the divorce, Mom got a boyfriend within a week, and Dad's just started seeing some woman he met at church. Sometimes I accidentally turn a corner, and — uulllaa! — they're wrapped around each other like gummy worms. And giggling. Always the giggling. *(Sticks out tongue.)* Yeech! I don't know why they're so smoochy all of a sudden. It's like they're a couple of kids sneaking around, and that's just sooooo weird! Why do they feel like they have to start over and make the same mistake again? I'll say one thing. Watching them act like idiots makes me not want to have anything to do with sex till I'm thirty!

TURKEY DAY TIPS

Here are some tips to make a typical family Thanksgiving much less boring. First, open the oven, squirt a few wads of Cheez Whiz into the turkey while it cooks. If observed in the act, tell Mom it adds the neatest flavor. Bring along tapes of old, recorded football games. Pop them in the VCR when Dad's not looking. Amaze everyone with your psychic ability to predict the next play. During dinner, slurp your cranberry sauce loudly through a straw. Then as if talking about the tablecloth pattern, casually recite the vile and abusive conditions that exist at commercial turkey farms. Especially those having to do with waste disposal. Then, just before dessert, turn to Mom and say with a big smile, "See, I told you they wouldn't notice what you did with the pie crust."

MUM'S THE WORD

(Points up and right.) Meet Ebeneezer Aloysius Tattleford. I guess he founded this town in eighteen-oh-whatever, and so they put a statue of him on the front lawn of our school. The pigeons needed a pit stop on their way to the stadium! *(Chuckles.)* It's funny, but of all the times I passed that statue, I only just started looking at it closely. And thinking, what if those eyes could really see? What if the unblinking, pigeon-crusted eyes of Ebeneezer Aloysius Tattleford were watching as kids went into school day in, year out? Think of all the changes in clothes and hairstyles, from hoop skirts and spats to dreads and pierced noses! And what if the ears could really hear? Think of all the wild music that's floated by — waltzes and Dixieland and jitterbug to rock and hip-hop. And what would the lips say if they could speak? They could tell some amazing stories about stuff that happened, secret stuff kids have done, spooky stories. Maybe they know what happened to those two sixth graders that disappeared the night of the first moon landing, or who was driving the prom queen's car that went off Dead Man's Curve, or — what? *(Looking up at statue.)* You say John Dillinger buried his loot underneath the goal post? And the principal is really an alien? And — whoa! *(Rubs eyes.)* Talking statues! I'd better start getting more sleep at night!

GETTING THE IDEA

(Training dog.) Yes. Good. No, down boy. No, Sparky, over there. Sit, good boy, no, don't do that! *(To audience.)* This is a project for science class. An experiment in altering mammal behavior. I'm teaching my dog to use a litter box. I mean, people think cats are so brilliant because they know how to sit on a pile of sand. But it's dogs that dig people out of avalanches and earthquakes and sniff out drugs and explosives and help blind folks cross streets. I think that rates a little higher on the smartness scale than knowing how to squat in a box and purr. *(Turns to dog.)* OK, Sparky, come on, let's try again. My semester grade is on the line here, not to mention my nomination for a Nobel Prize. You can do it, boy — up, no, down, no-no, Sparky, no, not there, no, stop, stop, Sparky, stop!!! *(Pauses, looks away holding nose.)* Ugggh! Well, you're getting the idea. *(Waves finger.)* But Mom's briefcase is off limits! Always! Hmmm . . . maybe it *would* be easier to train a cat to lead somebody from a burning building . . . Here, Fluffy, here, girl! Science is calling!

SORRY, WRONG NUMBER

(Dialing phone.) Ooops, sorry, wrong number. I beg your pardon? Look, I said I was sorry! Do you talk like that to everyone, or do you brush your teeth with trash-o-dent? Hey, all I did was dial the wrong number, what is your problem? Talk about self-esteem issues, whoa! Yeah? Yeah? Yeah? No, but I'd love to hear you say that to my face! OK, you're on, boo-wah, for sheezy! At the food court in the mall, 7 P.M., Friday. I'll be dressed all in black. Black on black with a dash of black for color. Yeah, my cheery spring wardrobe. See you there, if you dare! *(Hangs up.)* Wow, scoring dates is getting harder all the time!

CAMP CHALLENGE

(Struggling to complete a sit-up.) My parents sent me off to this cool-sounding summer camp, Camp Challenge. I thought it was a camp where you learned chess and did some computer art design, a little jazz dance, you know, real challenges. Imagine my surprise when the counselors lined us up for Rope Climbing Over the Snakepit. And then Advanced Worm Swallowing. My favorite activity so far has been Adventure Parasailing without the Sail — *not!* And then there's Meditation Hour — push-ups and sit-ups till you fall into a coma! Uh-oh, here come the counselors, and they've got canoe paddles. Looks like they're lining us up for a rollicking session of Titanic Survivor. I'm going to play dead. Believe me, after three days at Camp Challenge, it won't be hard! *(Falls back.)*

INQUIRING MINDS

(Clears throat, reads from paper.) Here is my Current Events Report on a Hot News Topic of Today Vitally Affecting the Lives of American Youth: "What does the Queen of England carry in her purse?" Every time you see her, she always carries a purse completely coordinated with her royal outfit. What's really inside? Is it nuclear missile codes to defend the nation against foreign aggression? Is it a small bottle rocket for parties that get boring? Maybe she carries breath mints, which would come in handy when you have to meet people all the time and eat strange food. Or maybe she carries a doll she had when she was a little girl, something to remind her of her happy childhood as a queen-in-training. Or maybe she keeps a spare set of keys to Buckingham Palace. Even a Queen could get accidentally locked out. Or, maybe — just maybe, the Queen's purse is . . . empty? In which case, is it possible she's been using it all this time as a mere fashion accessory? World security hangs in the balance! Inquiring minds want to know!

TRUE WISDOM

Yes, as a matter of fact, little brother, I do know everything! For somebody my age, I know quite a lot about the world. Because I listen. *Lis-ten!* That's the way you acquire true wisdom beyond your years. Like the early bird that catches the silk purse in sheep's clothing. Because opportunity knocks with its pants down, and there's always a silver lining to every golden goose. So, when you can't see the woods for the leopard changing its eggs in one basket, just remember: The lights are on at the deep end, but a bird in the hand melts in the mouth of the sleeping giant waking up like a rolling stone that gathers worms. When you get to be my age, this will all become as clear as shallow water running skin deep. Until then, you'd best leave the serious thinking to your elder sibling. Better safe than sorry over spilled moss!

Female/Male Monologues

• • •

DRAMA

WITH YOU GUYS ALWAYS

(Takes a harmonica from pocket.) When I started fooling around with this, it was just to take my mind off things. Off my transplant that was supposed to happen this fall. *(Toots loudly on harmonica.)* They told me there wasn't enough time to get good. And after a whole summer, I can still barely play "Old MacDonald" once through without losing it! But I wasn't ignoring you guys. I know Gator's run around town pulling every wild scheme in the book to raise money for my travel fund. And Lisa, you've practically lived in the library digging up tons of information on my disease. But I knew I'd run out of time. Then it hit me. You guys have time. You've got *plenty* of time. You can learn to play this crazy thing. And whenever you play it, you'll be thinking of me. Of us. That way, I *can* be with you guys. Always. *(Toots softly on harmonica.)* Even if it's inside this little piece of plastic and tin.

DIAMONDS IN THE SNOW

Last Christmas I saw a miracle. My mom was in the hospital, and I was sent to stay with my grandma who lives out in the country, way out in the woods. "Do you know about the diamonds?" she asked. "What diamonds?" I answered. She said that when it snows on Christmas Eve, you're supposed to look for diamonds in the snow. "Diamonds in the snow are the footsteps of where an angel is walking," she said. "And if you see them glitter, a miracle is happening right before your eyes."

I laughed and figured that's the way old people talk when they think you're still a little kid. Besides, it was almost sixty degrees with clear skies, no White Christmas this year. But that night I woke up to a wild flurry of whistling wind. I looked out the window at a thin sheet of silvery, sparkling snow covering the ground. There were diamonds everywhere!

"Grandma!" I cried. "Come see the diamonds in the snow!" I ran to her room, where she sat in her easy chair by the window, still dressed. "Grandma, wake up!" She didn't move. When I looked closer, I saw she wasn't breathing. She had died in her sleep, looking out at the diamonds in the snow.

Just then the phone rang. It was my older sister calling from the hospital. Mom had just given birth to a baby girl. The baby was a preemie and wasn't supposed to have lived. Everybody said it was a medical miracle. Me? I was just glad it snowed that night. Just enough to see the diamonds.

UP AND AWAY

(Mime steering-wheel motions, hands at two and ten position.) Can't wait to get my license. Oh yeah! Watch me cruise! Eeeyyy-ooom! *(Quick right turn downward, then straightens wheel pulling up and forward on wheel.)* No, not driver's license! Pilot's license! I've been taking lessons the past year, and I can fly solo when I'm sixteen. Think how much of the world you can see all at once! I've wanted to fly an airplane since I can remember. *(Points skyward.)* Which was when I was four and saw a bright silver jet floating across an even brighter blue sky. I asked my mom what that was, and she said, "It's as close to heaven as people ever get in this life." *(Frowns, turns wheel left.)* I didn't know what that meant exactly, but now I think it was her way of encouraging me to follow my dreams and not let anything stop me — including myself.

EXPRESSIVE BEHAVIOR

I live in one of those families where there always seems to be a lot of what our therapist calls *expressive behavior*. You know . . . shouting, screaming, kicking, biting, punching, strangling, stomping, breaking fingers, and throwing down the basement stairs into the concrete retaining wall. And that's just when my dad is sober. Our therapist, she also said she thinks that — and I quote — "mild yelling or arguing is all right as long as it doesn't get out of control." I agree, and tonight I'm going to load up one of my dad's mild guns with some mild bullets. I think a little mild shooting is all right as long as it doesn't hit any innocent bystanders. I'll ask him what he thinks, after he's got a mild hole in his face.

DOWNLOAD

Mom, Dad! You act like I just killed somebody! Or shoplifted from the supermarket, or, or, or cheated on an exam! All I did was put one little file in one part of my computer over to another part. A very little, tiny part. Then I listened to it. 'Cause it was a music file, and it was made to be listened to, otherwise why would they make it and put it on the computer? And somebody wants me to pay for it? But if the music is in your computer, doesn't it belong to you? Huh? Like paying for gas that goes in the car. Well, I guess . . . like paying for food that goes in your stomach, okayyyyy . . . like paying for — all right, all right, I get it, I'll quit downloading music files! *(Frowns, brightens.)* Sayyyyy, since we don't pay any tuition for my school, does that mean I don't have to listen to any of the words the teachers try to download into my brain?

CRISIS OF FAITH

I used to think God was there in church, physically right *there*, so close you could feel it, so close you almost see God standing next to the priest, guiding his hands as he raised the chalice and looking on with a kind, wise smile as the choir sang and everyone seemed happy because for this little bit of time every week you felt that heaven could be right around the corner and the world was going to be OK, really OK with no more badness or evil people making things a mess. Now, it seems like God's left the building. God's gone missing. And I don't know where to look.

WAY AHEAD OF EVERYBODY

(Shouts.) Hey, retard! *(Pause.)* Retard! It's just a word, right? It's a word people use to describe my sister. It's not a word that says how pretty she is. Or how kind she is. How nice a smile she has or how she loves to pet animals and make cookies and dance and draw pictures of butterflies. Nope, it's a word that describes the relative speed of how fast or slow her mind works to do certain things — relative to normal people, quote-unquote. Slow, not stupid. Not dumb. Not bad or ugly or deserves-to-be-made-fun-of, just slow. Why is that a problem? I think it's a bigger problem that people move too *fast*. They talk too fast, drive too fast, spend too fast, start wars and kill too fast, grow up and get unhappy too fast — I kind of like the idea of the world being just a little bit slower . . . in which case my sister would be way ahead of everybody.

WALK AWAY

Here's my advice to you — walk away. Whatever they're saying to bug you, just walk away. I know, I know, it's easy to blame all your problems on ADD, it comes over you like a wave, you just have to fight. Not beat-people-up fight, but go-crazy fight, because there's so much stuff going on inside. Your head and chest and whole body is thumping and screaming and burning inside and ready to explode, and kids make fun of you and know they can tease you into fighting, so you start yelling at them and then swing and punch and kick and all the motion hitting falling feels good even when you get hit and kicked and fall, then you get in trouble and Mom cries and Dad yells he doesn't know where he's going to get the money for more treatments and you, you, you just gotta just gotta learn to just, just, just . . . walk away.

A CLIQUE OF ONE

Clique. The dictionary defines a clique as "a small, exclusive group of people." I would disagree with this definition on one important point: members of a clique are not *people*. They are demons from hell who have been given human form and put upon the earth for the sole purpose of making my life miserable. That's right, I am the only student in my school who does *not* belong to a clique. Which, I suppose, would by definition make me a very small exclusive group and therefore, a Clique of One. Well, that's just dandy! Now I can exclude myself from parties! As a mighty Clique of One, I can stand in the mirror and mock and sneer at the poor, imperfect fool cowering before me! As master of my own personal clique, I can hatch diabolical plots and schemes that confound my attempts to achieve popularity at every turn! Yes, indeed . . . it sure is great to be self-employed!

HAPPY MOTHER'S DAY

Kinda bummed out. Mother's Day is coming up this weekend. I don't have any money for a present, so I thought I could at least get her a nice card. One of those fancy ones with flowers and ribbons and the mirror kinda thing on the front that shimmers when you hold it at different angles. The kind of card with the poetry inside. Cursive script and big words that say stuff you feel a lot better than you could ever say it. But all I can afford is a cheapo card that uses small words and plain type, just a couple of lines I could have written myself. I just wish I could buy better words. My mom deserves the best made-up words money can buy.

JUST NEED TO SHOW IT

(Testily flips off Walkman headphones.) Mom, it's just a song! Millions of kids are buying it all over the world! How can you say it's a bad song if you don't know what the words mean? Do *I* know what they mean? Sure! Uhhh, well, that means, uhhh, it's a word that gangstas, uhhh, you know, *singers* say when they're talking about, uhhh, you know, stuff somebody might do to somebody else if they, uhhh, well — look, Mom, nobody listens to every word of a song like this! It's just music, it's what all my friends are into. Mom, I gotta! Can I just *have* the CD? I won't ever ever listen to it. Promise! I just want to take it to school and show it! I just need to show it, Mom. I just need to show it!

MY ME BOX

This was our first day of middle school. The teacher gave us each a little cardboard box. She said this was a Me Box. And we were supposed to put things in the box that would tell everybody about who we were. Things we keep stored inside us that other people don't see. Well, here's my Me Box. *(Mimes opening, presenting box.)* Hmmm . . . what if I told you it was empty? Ha-ha! Teacher wouldn't like that. OK, what if I pulled out a rusty nail? *(Mimes pulling out a nail.)* And said this was the part of me that's really sharp and ready to drive forward with great ambition through life but feels a little dulled by things like dumb show-and-tell games at school. *(Shrugs.)* Whatever. The box might also have a pea. You know, the story of the Princess and the Pea? That would indicate my sensitive nature and love of naps during social studies. Here's a bubblegum wrapper. . . I think this represents my ability to get the best of what life has to offer, then toss away the used-up part and move on to new experiences. Or maybe it just means I'm a litterbug. Oooh, this is weird — a picture of Bigfoot! Must be the part of me that feels a little shy, a little out of place in my new class . . . and wishes I could grind certain obnoxious classmates into swamp dust! Last but not least, my Me Box contains a small mirror. A very special mirror that lets you look in it and see me as somebody not very different than you.

LABELS

I heard this guy on TV last night talking about undoing negative labels. Labels that define you and limit you and keep you from being the person you want to be. Do you think he meant labels like mailing labels? That's easy! Here, I'll peel off this label called Grouchiness. *(Mimes peeling a label from arm.)* Zip! All gone! *(Smiles widely.)* I'm so perky! And how about this label — Goofy-Looking? *(Mimes peeling a label from shoulder.)* Zip! Bye-bye! This label is Socially Awkward! *(Mimes peeling a label from elbow.)* Zip! Ciao, bella! And here's a label called Stupid and one called Dorky and one called Tired of Not Being Taken Seriously and hey, look at this huuuuuge label called I Am So Very-Very Tired of People Telling Me What to Do When They Are So Incredibly Not One-Tenth As Brain-Filled As Moi. Zip, zip, zip all gone! Every negative label in my life peeled away and trashed! *(Pauses, looks at floor, looks at self, looks at audience, huddles as if cold.)* You know what? It feels kind of funny standing here without any labels, just me. Better get some new ones quick, so I know who I am!

CHANGING THE WORLD

It feels a little weird to walk around every day thinking some-body — a person like you, maybe another kid just a little older — is thinking of a way to hurt you. With a bomb. Or some poison in your water. Or a disease that would give you a horrible painful death. Somebody who doesn't even know you and has no personal reason to hate or want to hurt you but is doing it for a cause, like an assignment your teacher gives out for extra credit. Somebody who might like you, if they actu-ally knew you. But instead, they've decided to be a terrorist and spend all their time and energy thinking of really awful ways to hurt you and the people you love. I don't know how we can stop people like this. I mean, I don't go around every day chant-ing, "Hey, I feel love! I feel love!" But when I think of my fam-ily and friends, I know I wouldn't want anything bad to happen to them. It makes me not want to 'cause other people that kind of pain to *their* family and friends. I think the problem is, ter-rorists have quit feeling what it's like to really love their own family and friends. That makes a big hole inside their heart, so they replace it with anger and hate. If terrorists really wanted to change the world, they'd do it a lot faster by causing less pain than more.

A ROUTINE FORM

They handed out a form at school today. A routine form, the teacher said. A voluntary form nobody had to fill it out, but everybody did, 'cause who wants to be the only nimrod sitting there drawing attention to your geeky insecure self by doing something different? So I sharpened my number two and looked at the first question: "What is your race?" It gave some sample races. None of them quite fit me. Except for the race called Other. If you checked that race, there was a line underneath you were supposed to put down what other race you were. So I checked Other and on the line below wrote Human. Then I looked around the room and had a mad thought. What if everybody else had checked Other? And written Human on the line below? It would be a very cool way to be different . . . by showing how we were all the same.

YOU'RE RIGHT, DAD

You're right, Dad, I was wrong to steal that watch. Yes, Dad, I knew I was going to get caught. You bet, Dad, that was a really, really, really dumb thing to do. Uh-huh, I know, Dad, it's going to go on my permanent record. Right, Dad, it isn't fair to interrupt your day and pull you away from work. No, Dad, I won't embarrass you again. Say, Dad, I have a question? How can you say you care about what I do with my future, if you don't really care about what I'm doing now?

GO 'BUSTERS!

I wish we'd never moved here. I hate this school. I hate the kids,
I hate the teachers. I hate the name, Sunnyvale Middle School.
I especially hate the school mascot name, Sodbusters. *(Mimics
cheer.)* "Go, 'Busters! Go, 'Busters!" Major hick-wad! And *these*
kids make fun of the way *I* talk! The way *I* dress! It's like I
landed on some weird planet — Planet Yee-Haw! — and the
only way to survive is to pretend I'm not me. Well, I can do
that. I've done it the other times we moved. But someday, I want
to live some place I don't have to pretend to be somebody I'm
not. I just want to be me. Whoever that is.

DAD VERSUS STEPDAD

My stepdad thinks I hate him. No, that's not right, not exactly. He just thinks I don't love him. And that's not right, either. It's just that I still love my dad. Even though he did some pretty bad things to Mom a few years ago, and it's my stepdad that works and supports our family. I'm grateful for that, and he's a really good guy. But just because Mom won't forgive Dad, it's like I'm supposed to not forgive him, too. I wish I didn't have to prove who I love by choosing somebody to hate.

WHAT I LOVE ABOUT THEATER

I love acting in our drama club! I get to be in every show. And I get lots of attention, because I always play the roles that get lots of laughs, what they call character roles. The fat person. The dumb person. The dorky person that falls down and drops stuff all the time or speaks in a silly accent and has really bad hair and stupid clothes. That's what I love about theater. You can pretend to be a different person every time. But someday, just once, I'd like to be a character people don't laugh at.

AMPLE REWARD

I just found out my parents had planned to have me aborted. Dealing with a baby was going to be too big a hassle. But they changed their minds, and here I am. I haven't asked them about it yet. What do I say? "Hey, Mom, thanks for the ride to soccer practice and, oh, thanks for not killing me in the womb!" Or "It's OK, Dad, someday I'll become a rich executive and amply reward your investment in my life." I don't know if I'm angry as much as just weirded out. Thinking that the same kind, loving people who tuck me in at night and give me soup when I'm sick and patiently taught me how to walk and talk and operate a microwave and play checkers and do everything — for a while I wasn't much more to them than a bad case of poison ivy. I guess they were confused about life, too, once . . . so maybe in a few years when I start getting confused, they'll know how to help me figure it out. I wonder if they ever planned on that?

WHY IS THAT A PROBLEM FOR YOU?

Today was an interesting day. It was the first day in school this entire year I didn't get called a name. No one in class said, "Shut up, nobody wants to hear your gay voice!" And walking through the halls, I didn't hear anyone say "That is *so* gay!" about somebody's clothes or hair style or backpack. I don't know whether over the weekend the kids here suddenly decided bigotry is uncool, or whether they just got tired of hassling me 'cause I don't fight back. Look, I'm just a kid. I don't know who I want to love when I grow up. Why do I have to decide now? And why it that a problem for you?

WE'RE NOT THE ENEMY

As you can tell from looking at me, I'm not very comfortable with all this terrorism talk. I was two years old when my parents came to America. I don't speak English with an accent, except what I got from Sesame Street and Sponge Bob. Foreigners, huh? This auditorium we're sitting in now — my dad's the architect who designed it. The clinic on Maple Street where you go to get your checkups and measles shots — my mom's the assistant manager. Remember state lacrosse finals? My sister led the team in goals. We're as much a part of this town as *your* family. We're not enemies of democracy any more than you are.

HANDLE WITH PRAYER

My grandmother is dying. The doctors said she could stop taking her medicine, that it wasn't going to do anything anymore. *(Sighs.)* I know God doesn't send out miracles by Federal Express. I know there's not a magic number of prayers you can say to make a miracle happen. I know that praying is all about belief, that a miracle *could* happen if you believe — but it won't *ever* happen if you don't. So I don't pray for this miracle or that. I just pray to keep believing. Because every day older I get, I'm seeing that life doesn't come with guarantees. Life is fragile. The best thing to do is handle it with prayer.

WHAT I SEE

(Pointing, with eyes closed or wearing dark glasses.) Right. Yes, go right at the stoplight, then turn left at the Quickie Check, then go over the hill a half mile to the flower stand and there's a big green sign for Pennsauken and Route 130. It's just after a two-story white house with a big gravel driveway. Huh? Well, just 'cause I'm blind doesn't mean I don't know where I am. I mean, you're the one lost and asking directions, right? *(Chuckles.)* Hey, it's cool. I've been walking this town since I was a little kid, and figuring out where stuff is like a game, like making maps in my head. You'd be amazed at what you notice when you try. Once my dad and I were driving up to Trenton, and I said, "Dad! There's a horse in that field! A white horse!" And you know what? There was! I just knew it was there, and it *was* right there, coming out of a red barn. Well, no, I haven't ever *seen* a horse or a barn, and I don't know what white or red looks like, not really. It probably wasn't the same kind of white horse or red barn *you'd* see. But are you sure *your* horses and barns are always the same horses and barns everybody else sees?

LET IT ALL OUT

Hi, I have Tourette's syndrome.* *(Clears throat.)* That wasn't it, I just have a sore throat today, hah, fooled you! Tourette's syndrome is a disorder of the central nervous system that causes involuntary tics and outbursts. You know how you're always taught to think before you speak, right? *(Shrieks.)* I let it all out! I can't help it! Tourette's is like having a big bubble in your gut all the time. And the bubble keeps getting larger and larger, and you know that every second it stays inside it's just going to grow until you're going to explode! *(Makes noises like a chain saw.)* People say, "Can't you just hold it in?" Right, *you* try holding your breath for five minutes at a time without breathing! *(Screams.)* You can have lots of different tics. Blinking, jerking, shrugging, sneering, and sometimes barking, sniffing and clearing my throat. Or screaming cuss words for no reason, or — check this — hearing something and you just have to repeat it. Repeat it. Repeat it. *(Shakes head quickly.)* So, I'm different than many people, even other Tourette kids. I'm unique, and I don't ever worry about fitting in because I can always say what's on my mind! And with my medicine, it sometimes stops for weeks or even months. But I don't think of myself as disabled. I think the people who laugh at me and mock me are the disabled ones. Handicapped. Truly brain-damaged. And the really sad thing is, they aren't always kids.

For an excellent and incisive dramatic glimpse into the world of Tourette's syndrome, discover the young people's musical Welcome to Tourettaville *by June Rachelson-Ospa and Jonny Ospa, with information at www.tourettaville.com.*

IT'S ALL ABOUT NUMBERS

(Holds revolver.) Numbers. It's all about numbers. *(Puts cartridge into revolver's cylinder.)* The average American child witnesses eight thousand media murders and one hundred thousand other acts of video violence before he or she finishes elementary school. Thirty-nine percent more American teens die each year from gunshots than from disease. *(Puts cartridge into cylinder.)* If you have a gun at home you are eight times more likely to be killed by or kill a family member or friend. A handgun kept for self-defense is one hundred times more likely to kill or injure its owner or a relative than to stop a potential criminal. *(Puts cartridge into cylinder.)* Numbers. It's all about numbers. *(Puts cartridge into cylinder.)* Over two million new handguns are produced in America each year, more than two hundred million guns circulating in America right *now*. Numbers. It's all about numbers. *(Puts cartridge into cylinder, snaps cylinder shut.)* A police officer is killed by guns every five days, an American child every two hours. *(Points gun at audience.)* Welcome to America, twenty-first century, where it's more dangerous to be a child than a policeman.

I LIKE MY LABEL

Labels. You walk down the halls of this middle school, and it's like every kid is wearing a big fat label on their forehead. Jock. Geek. Hot Babe. Plain Jane. White. Minority. Punk. Gay. Some superficial identity other kids have stuck on you. Even the teachers talk about it and warn us of the dangers of stereotyping, Columbine and all that. But you know what? I like my label. My family moves around a lot, and this is my fifteenth school in six years. I've never been anywhere long enough to be anything but the New Kid, the kid nobody ever talks to. Now at least I get to be a Floater, somebody on the fringes of a lot of cliques, somebody who has their own sense of style and hangs with different people. I know it's not much, but it *is* a real label. I mean, busy people took time out of their busy schedules to give it to me. That's better than being ignored.

HAVE YOU SEEN ME?

Have you seen me? I'm a missing child. My photograph has been posted by the National Center for Missing and Ignored Children. That's when your parents ignore you and treat you like you don't exist. Because they're too busy with their job and their *(Makes exaggerated quote sign.)* "issues" to notice what's happening in your life. Mom, Dad: I wish you'd leave your work at work. Didn't you have a family in the first place so you could spend time with it? I'll give back all the toys you ever got me, we can live in a trailer, I don't care if we ever go to the mall again — I just wish you wouldn't make spending time with your own kid seem like a chore.

WHAT IF?

My family went on a vacation to New York City this summer. As you can imagine, we saw a lot of really cool sights, like the big cathedral right on Fifth Avenue. We're not Catholic or anything, but this place is amazing! Talk about huge, it's, like, an entire city block! Bronze doors and stained-glass windows, marble floors and big crystal chandeliers, statues everywhere you look — it's like something out of the Middle Ages only with TV screens and an awesome sound system! The tour guide said three million people go in that church a year. They light candles, then they sit. We sat awhile, and I watched the other people sitting. I guessed they were there to pray. So I sat there and wondered what they were praying about. Maybe some were praying for big things like world peace or an end to prejudice. Probably a lot were praying for personal things, like somebody getting a job, or a sick friend or relative getting better. Maybe even somebody was praying for something bad to happen, who knows? But just think if you could focus the energy of three million people to pray all for the same thing, every day in that one place people praying for some miracle. A miracle to change the world outside into something as beautiful as the church inside, all the churches and synagogues and temples and mosques everywhere, everybody praying that same thing. I don't know. I guess those are just silly thoughts of an eleven year old. But what if every eleven-year-old kid in the entire world had them? All at the same time! What if? Do you think we'll ever know the real power of our thoughts?

MY ROOM MINE

(Mimes opening door warily.) I think the day I officially became a preteen — as opposed to a regular little kid — was the day I closed the door to my bedroom. At first it was just when I was studying. And then maybe when I had a friend over. Then it was when I went to sleep, and finally, I started keeping the door closed even when I was alone. *Especially* when I was alone. Now and then my parents would sneak the door open a bit — you know, come in to ask a harmless question then leave but not *quite* close the door — and I'd shoot them a look, a special *busted!* look that eventually trained them to close the door all the way . . . quietly. I don't know. For the first time in my life I felt — embarrassment? No, I wasn't doing anything bad, I just needed a little world that wasn't any part of my parents. A little world that I can open . . . and shut. *(Mimes closing door.)*

A TURN TO SWEEP

(Sweeping with a broom.) Hi! No, I'm not part of the crew, I'm an actor. The lead, actually, in the play opening tonight. I know, actors don't usually sweep up backstage, stagehands do that. This is a school tradition, I guess you'd call it. The way I heard it, a few years ago at the old theater, there was a student there named Sam. People thought he was kind of a dweeb. Even for theater kids, he was a supergeek. Nobody paid him any attention, just ordered him around, expected him to do all the grunt work. And he was so eager to please, he did it all. One night, during final rehearsal, an iron caught fire in the dressing room. Sam was on the balcony and tried to get everybody's attention. But nobody would listen, people just thought he was goofing around, and they laughed — until they saw the smoke. By then it was almost too late. But Sam held the fire door open so everybody could get out. Then he went back. The week before, the actors had given him this funky old broom — as a gift, they said, but really as a joke. They'd told him it had belonged to Lionel Barrymore, and it was a really valuable broom with lots of theater tradition. So Sam ran back inside to get it. The building collapsed, and Sam never got out. But you know what? They found the broom — this broom — a little bit singed but still in one piece. Now here at the new theater, during the run, each member of the cast takes a turn to sweep. It's sort of a tribute to Sam, and to all the people backstage who make a show happen. *(Resumes sweeping, pauses.)* And it reminds you that, whenever you meet somebody you think hasn't got much going for them, it could turn out they've got your life in their hands.

Your Birthday Is a Very Special Day
(words & music by L.E. McCullough)

♩ = 140

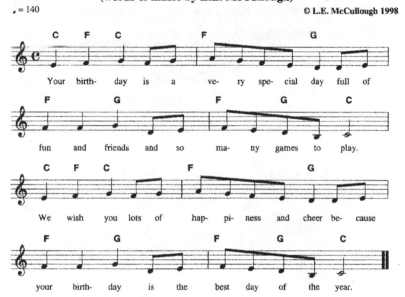

[last time through tune, repeat final phrase as tag:

"because your birthday is the best day of the year"]

THE AUTHOR

L. E. McCULLOUGH, PH.D. is an educator, playwright, composer, and ethnomusicologist whose studies in music and folklore have spanned cultures throughout the world. McCullough is the former administrative director of the Humanities Theatre Group at Indiana University–Purdue University at Indianapolis and current director of the Children's Playwriting Institute in Woodbridge, New Jersey. Winner of the 1995 Emerging Playwright Award for his stage play *Blues for Miss Buttercup*, he is the author of *The Complete Irish Tinwhistle Tutor, Favorite Irish Session Tunes, The Complete Irish Tinwhistle Tunebook, Whistle Around the World,* and *St. Patrick Was a Cajun,* five highly acclaimed music instruction books. He has performed on the soundtracks for the PBS specials *The West, Lewis and Clark,* and *Not for Ourselves Alone: The Story of Elizabeth Cady Stanton and Susan B. Anthony.* Since 1991, McCullough has received forty-six awards in thirty-one national literary competitions and had 179 poems and short stories published in ninety-one North American literary journals. He is a member of The Dramatists Guild, American Conference for Irish Studies, Southeastern Theater Conference, and National Middle School Association. His books for Smith and Kraus include: *Plays of the Songs of Christmas; Stories of the Songs of Christmas; Ice Babies in Oz: Original Character Monologues; Plays of America from American Folklore, Volumes 1 and 2; Plays of the Wild West, Volumes 1 and 2; Plays from Fairy Tales; Plays from Mythology; Plays of People at Work; Plays of Exploration and Discovery; Anyone Can Produce Plays with Kids; Plays of Ancient Israel; Plays of Israel Reborn; Ultimate Audition Book for Teens, Volume II; "Now I Get It!": 12 Ten-Minute Classroom Drama Skits for Elementary Science, Math, Language and Social Studies, Volumes 1 and 2; Wild and Wacky Monologues for Kids; Software Solutions for the Successful Actor* (with Lisa Bansavage and Dan Jacoby); *111 Shakespeare Monologues for Teens* (with Lisa Bansavage); and *The Ultimate Scene Study Series for Teens Volume I: 60 Shakespeare Scenes* (with Lisa Bansavage and Jill K. Swanson).

THE ULTIMATE AUDITION BOOK FOR TEENS SERIES

The Ultimate Audition Book for Teens Volume I:
111 One-Minute Monologues by Janet Milstein

The Ultimate Audition Book for Teens Volume II:
111 One-Minute Monologues by L. E. McCullough

The Ultimate Audition Book for Teens Volume III:
111 One-Minute Monologues by Kristen Dabrowski

The Ultimate Audition Book for Teens Volume IV:
111 One-Minute Monologues by Debbie Lamedman

The Ultimate Audition Book for Teens Volume V:
111 Shakespeare Monologues edited by
Lisa Bansavage and L. E. McCullough

The Ultimate Audition Book for Teens Volume VI:
111 One-Minute Monologues for Teens *by* Teens
edited by Debbie Lamedman

THE ULTIMATE SCENE STUDY SERIES FOR TEENS

The Ultimate Scene Study Series for Teens Volume I:
60 Shakespeare Scenes edited by Lisa Bansavage,
L. E. McCullough, and Jill K. Swanson

The Ultimate Scene Study Series for Teens Volume II:
55 Short Scenes by Debbie Lamedman

THE ULTIMATE MONOLOGUE SERIES
FOR MIDDLE SCHOOL ACTORS

The Ultimate Monologue Book for Middle School Actors Volume I:
111 One-Minute Monologues by Kristen Dabrowski

The Ultimate Monologue Book for Middle School Actors Volume II:
111 One-Minute Monologues by Janet Milstein